Close Like A Boss
A Problem Solver's Guide For Consistent Lesson Closure

SEAN CAIN

DEDICATION

This book is dedicated to the teachers who shared the roadblocks they face when trying to adopt a new instructional practice. I admire their effort and celebrate their success.

CONTENTS

ACKNOWLEDGMENTS

The author would like to acknowledge Lesa Cain and Tricia Tsang. This book is better due to their support and contributions.

INTRODUCTION

The Fundamental 5 represent the five high-yield instructional practices that leverage every other high-yield practice a teacher can use in the classroom. These are the practices that exceedingly effective teachers use at higher frequency and better quality than typical teachers. This pattern of practice was observed and recognized by a team of educators led by Sean Cain and shared in the books **The Fundamental 5: The Formula for Quality Instruction** (2011), written by Sean Cain and Mike Laird, and **The Fundamental 5 Revisited: Exceptional Instruction in Every Setting** (2021), written by Sean Cain, Mike Laird, Sherilynn Cotten, and Jayne Ellspermann. The five practices are:

- Frame the Lesson
- Recognize and Reinforce
- Frequent, Small Group, Purposeful Talk About the Learning
- Critical Writing
- Work in the Power Zone

All five practices are critical, essential, and are part of a cohesive body of fundamentally sound pedagogy. The practices work best when used together, and to ignore one or more of **The Fundamental 5** practices is detrimental to students. However, if there is a *Fundamental 1*—a first among equals—that practice is Lesson Framing *with* Appropriate Lesson Closure.

Why is this the case? Closing the Lesson appropriately is one of the most powerful retention strategies available to teachers. It is a practice that exemplary teachers use consistently, and typical teachers consistently skip. Over the past ten years, in the course of tens of thousands of classroom visits by the author and the Lead Your School (LYS) team, only about 5% of teachers are observed Closing their Lessons consistently and appropriately.[1] This is a depressingly low number, especially when one considers that close to 500,000 teachers have at least held a copy of **The Fundamental 5** in their hands.

For experienced school leaders, the fact that providing staff with a book on better instruction is not the best vehicle for changing teacher practice is not surprising. Been there, done that. They know that embedded, ongoing staff development is the key. Or is it? The LYS team also observes teachers at schools who have received quality, practical training on the practice of Lesson Framing with Appropriate Lesson Closure. The

---

[1] Lead Your School (LYS): A confederation of education leaders that work with schools across the country for the sole purpose of optimizing outcomes for all students. LYS was founded by Robert "Bob" Brezina, E. Don Brown, and Sean Cain.

numbers move but not dramatically, inching up from 5% to a modest 15%. Even more curious is the fact that as the teachers who Close their Lessons consistently begin to experience significant, measurable improvements in student performance, their peers still do not take notice or engage.

Out of a combination of inquisitiveness and frustration, LYS gathered a focus group of teachers to try to get to the bottom of what prevents a teacher from implementing the practice of Lesson Framing with Appropriate Lesson Closure correctly and consistently. The group of teachers selected were purposefully *not* a random and representative sample of the overall teacher population. The selected teachers were all:

1. Hard working and dedicated.
2. Demonstrating a level of success teaching at-risk student populations.
3. Trained on the practice of Lesson Framing with Appropriate Lesson Closure.
4. NOT Closing their lessons consistently and appropriately.

In short, the focus group was made up of some of the best of the 95% of teachers who just cannot or will not do an identified solid gold, sure fire, and blue chip best practice. These teachers were asked, **"Why don't you Close your Lessons?"**

This book shares what these teachers told us, and the answers we shared with them. This is messy and real life. If Lesson Framing with Appropriate Lesson Closure was easy to implement, every teacher would do it. The overwhelming evidence shows us that this simple-on-paper, high-yield instructional strategy is not easy in practice. The evidence also shows us that when the practice is implemented correctly and consistently, it can significantly improve student performance. When LYS trained teachers are honest in their attempts to work hard and serve students, then we at LYS do everything in our power to make sure that the hard work of these teachers is transformed into increased levels of student success. This is why we at LYS keep searching for practical, scalable solutions for teachers.

It should go without saying that with Lesson Closure, as is the case for every other powerful teacher practice, there is no 100% expectation. No teacher can do every high-yield instructional practice 100% of the time. The classroom is dynamic and unpredictable. Sometimes life just happens. However, with appropriate Lesson Closure, any observed frequency less than 90% means that significant levels of student performance and potential are being left untapped.

For an in-depth discussion of Lesson Framing with Appropriate Lesson Closure, the reader should refer to **The Fundamental 5 Revisited: Exceptional Instruction in Every Setting** (2021), written by Cain, Laird, Cotten, and Ellspermann. Briefly, appropriate Lesson Closure occurs in the last three-to-five minutes of the class period. During this time at the end of the lesson (or lesson period) every student articulates the critical understanding or connections of the lesson *in their own words*. The primary vehicles for appropriate lesson Closure are the talking Close with a partner or a written Close. When the lesson is Closed correctly, the student is positioned to create a vibrant and robust memory of the most critical elements of the just completed lesson activities. Teachers who have students who retain more of what was previously taught are generally able to teach more new content. Over the course of a semester (or school year), students who are taught more content and retain more of what they were taught outperform students who are taught less content and retain less of what they were taught. It is a simple equation, driven by a slight change in pedagogy that most teachers continue to either overlook or outright avoid.

The teachers polled were honest and their reasons were legitimate. These are real constraints for teachers, and they are recognized as such. Fortunately, every one of the constraints can be, and have been, overcome. The reasons teachers provided for why they do not Close their Lessons cluster around common themes. The book is organized around those common themes. The solutions shared in this book are not "in a perfect world, this is what we would do" clichés that have little connection to actual classroom realities. This book is meant to be a practical educator resource, with proven suggestions that have been used to transition teachers into consistent Lesson Closers. To use this book, it is suggested that the reader scan the table of contents and find the reasons that are most aligned with their self-identified restraint(s). Our intent is that the responses to the selected Lesson Closure roadblocks will provide the reader with the strategies and/or insights that will help move them forward in their professional growth.

At LYS, every one of us is a public school educator and leader. We train (teach) teachers and school leaders across the country. With every one of the trainings (lessons) that we deliver, we Close that Lesson. This is one reason why LYS training and support are in demand—the knowledge shared in our training sticks...by design, even with Lesson Closure. The teachers we train retain the information about what to do, why it should be done, and how to do it. It is the actual doing, the *implementation*, that is the problem. Our goal is to solve the Lesson Closure implementation problem and for every teacher to...**Close Like A Boss!**

REASON 1:
I DO NOT HAVE TIME TO CLOSE THE LESSON

The feeling of not having enough time is legitimate. From an objective vantage point, today's teacher has more content to teach and less time to do it than yesterday's teacher. Today's teacher must teach prescribed content with embedded, rigorous performance standards that must be mastered in class periods that have been compressed to as short as 42 minutes. Today's classroom is not for the fearful, timid, and weak-willed. Based on the reality facing today's busy, over-stressed educator, we remind every teacher, "You do not have time to NOT Close your Lesson."

Consider the following common scenario. A teacher spends the entire lesson teaching and engaging students in their daily academic work until the bell rings. In this class, a great deal of academic stuff and things were completed. Upon closer inspection, what was actually accomplished? With great urgency, the teacher crammed a lot of information into one ear of the student. That information swirled around the student's brain where a large portion of the information seemingly evaporates. Then the bell rings and the student leaves the class to go to six to eight other classes before they return to the class in question the next day. At the beginning of next day's class, the teacher realizes that any information they thought was retained from the day before has evidently leaked out the student's other ear. The teacher's students do not quite remember what they did the day before, so the teacher is forced to reteach a chunk of yesterday's information. The time spent teaching yesterday's information (which seems to expand exponentially) reduces the amount of class time available to teach today's new content. This cycle repeats itself, day after day. Every day, the teacher gets a little more off pace, and the required content finish line becomes a little further out of reach.

However, if the teacher Closes the Lesson appropriately, the above-described situation changes. The teacher still crams a lot of information into one of the student's ears with great urgency. That information swirls around the student's brain where a lot of the information seemingly evaporates. But every day in this class, during the last three-to-five minutes of the period, the teacher has students articulate the **key understanding** of the lesson, either by talking to a partner or engaging in a quick critical writing exercise. By having students engage in one of these Closing activities, these students walk out of the class remembering more of what they were taught that day. The next day, because students remember more of what they were taught previously, the teacher does not have to reteach as much or for as long. This means they have more time to teach more new content, that students will remember because the teacher Closes every Lesson, every day. By the end of the year, this teacher, who Closes every lesson, every day, may not have taught all the required or desired content. But inevitably, they are miles ahead of the teacher who did not take time to Close their Lesson.

REASON 2:
I RUN OUT OF TIME TO CLOSE THE LESSON

Running out of time is a common reason teachers give for not Closing the Lesson. The teacher is busy teaching; students are busy working; and before the teacher realizes it, the bell rings, and the class is over. Period after period, day after day. The teacher wants to Close, plans to Close, but is surprised by the bell, and once again…no Closure.

This is a time management challenge. The reality of this situation is that within the actual class period most teachers do a poor job of managing time to the *exact* minute. This should not be construed as an indictment or personal flaw. It is simply a recognition of fact. During a class period, teachers manage a near infinite number of variables, make a near infinite number of micro-decisions, and teach complex, prescribed content. They do this as the clock continuously ticks, and their stress level increases throughout the day. Next to no one can consistently manage time in an adequate manner in such a setting. So what is the secret? How are a select few of our teachers able to manage time accurately enough to Close their Lessons consistently?

They use a timer. The teachers who Close their Lessons consistently use a timer. If a teacher is teaching a 47 minute class, they set their timer for 42 minutes. With the set timer now counting down, the teacher begins the day's instructional activities and quickly forgets about it. The timer then begins to chime 42 minutes later. The chime does not mean *talk faster.* The chime does not mean *work faster.* The chime means finish your thought *now* or tell the students to get to a stopping point *now.* It is *now* time for *all* students to engage in the Close. The use of a timer to facilitate Lesson Closure is such a critical component of the practice that when LYS trains teachers on Lesson Closure, a timer is provided. As emphasized in **The Fundamental 5 Revisited**, we can now unequivocally state, *No Timer = No Closure.*

REASON 3:
I FORGOT TO USE MY TIMER

The teacher plans to Close the Lesson. They have a timer to remind them to Close the Lesson. However, the teacher keeps forgetting to set the timer, which means that the teacher does not receive a cue to remind them to stop and Close the Lesson. This oversight results in yet another lesson not Closed. Even though this might sound a little silly, it is understandable. Existing habits getting in the way of new practice is simply part of the human condition. This can be frustrating for the teacher, but it is not insurmountable.

In the course of managing a class and delivering quality instruction, teachers have a million little things on their plate to prioritize, navigate, and execute. Asking the teacher to remember to use a timer is adding one more thing to their already overcrowded plate. No matter how helpful the intent, we (teacher, administrator, instructional coach, etc.) must admit that trying to remember to do one small new thing when a person is already operating at the edge of their capabilities in a high stress environment is, in a word, *difficult*.

The solution? The teacher does not need to try to remember to set and manage the timer. They are doing too much already. Instead they should do one of two things. One, the teacher could make setting and managing the timer a student job. At the beginning of every week, the teacher selects a student in each class to be the *timekeeper*. Tell the timekeeper that it is their responsibility to make sure that the class has time to engage in the Close. As soon as the timekeeper enters the classroom, they go to the timer, set it for the time of that period's Lesson Closure, and start the timer. This works in grades K-12. The job and the responsibility are neither too elementary nor too mature. This is just good practice.

Two, the teacher could download a programmable timer onto their computer. Then program multiple alarms that mirror the daily instructional schedule. For example, if first period ends at 8:55, then the teacher sets a Monday-Friday alarm for 8:50. When the timer goes off, the teacher stops the activity and Closes the Lesson. This should be done for each period the teacher is scheduled to teach. If the timer (alarm) can be displayed on the presentation board and counts down, it adds a sense of urgency and purpose to the classroom.

Do note that the author no longer recommends using the timer feature on a smart phone. Using a smart phone as a timer is a practice that is observed in some classrooms. When first adopted, this practice was considered effective. However, now the practice can be exceedingly distracting. Most smart phones constantly provide updates from sites that the teacher or student timekeeper uses. For example, ESPN, Facebook, Twitter, and Amazon, to name just a few, send numerous attention grabbing updates to mobile devices throughout the day. This has transformed smart phones into virtual information slot machines that are constantly paying out. These updates distract the person using the phone, making it more difficult to teach and support students (if it is the teacher) or stay attentive and focused on the learning activities (if it is the student). Regarding timers, simple and old fashioned are the best (least distracting) option.

REASON 4:
I FORGET TO COME UP WITH A CLOSE
OR I DID NOT PLAN FOR THE CLOSE

It was when teachers shared this reason for not Closing the Lesson that we knew that teachers were being completely transparent. All teachers have lessons that they deliver without doing the requisite planning that leads to a satisfying outcome. It is a real world reality that we loathe to admit.

Occasionally, forgetting to come up with and/or post a Close are understandable and forgivable. Sometimes *stuff* happens, and the teacher just has to get through today's lessons the best they can and hope that no one notices. On the other hand, regularly forgetting to create and/or post the Close either means that the teacher needs an improved planning routine, planning tool, posting routine, or that they simply do not value the practice. By reading this book, the assumption is that the reader values the practice. As such, let us focus on the planning tools and routines.

First, a Close should be part of every lesson plan. When planning a lesson, a teacher considers the content standard and the activities that best teach those standards. This is when the teacher should also consider what critical information and connections students should possess at the conclusion of the lesson and how they will articulate the connections and/or understanding.

Second, a prominent spot on the teacher's main presentation board should be designated for the Close. This brings us to a common, yet avoidable, problem observed in classrooms—presentation/white board overload. This is when there is so much information posted on the presentation board that (1) it overwhelms and confuses students, and (2) there is no room to prominently post the Lesson Frame. As a solution, it is suggested that teachers do the following (see the presentation board figures below). First, the teacher should clear everything from their presentation board and begin with a clean slate, as depicted in Figure A. Then the teacher should divide the presentation board into three, unequal areas, as depicted in Figure B.

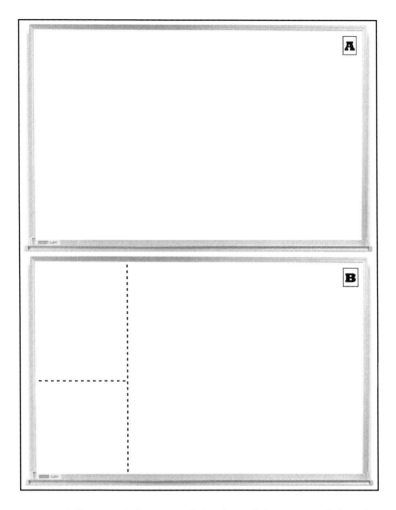

The top left area of the board is reserved for the Lesson Frame—*Objective* and *Close*. The space should be large enough where the Lesson Frame can be written at a size where it can be easily read, even from the back of the classroom. The slightly smaller, bottom left area of the

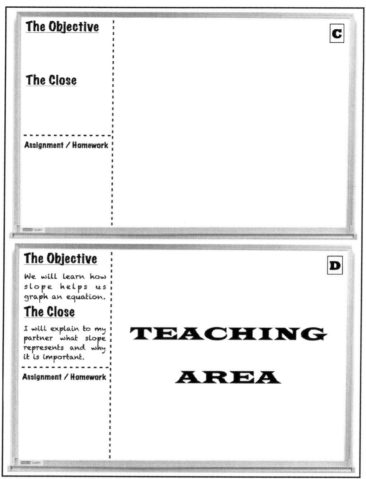

board is where the teacher posts today's assignment and homework information (see: Figure C). At the beginning of the day (or period), the teacher posts the Lesson Frame, writes down any pertinent assignment and homework information, and then uses the large open space on the right side of the board for modeling, demonstrating, and teaching today's lesson (see: Figure D). By adopting this board organizational model, the teacher removes less critical information from the board; is able to prominently post the Lesson Frame in the same place, every day; and has plenty of available space to teach today's lesson.

Teachers who Close their Lessons consistently (in all grades) inform their students early in the school year why the Close is important. These teachers explain to their students that they will engage in a Close every day, and they share the positive impact this will have on their learning. These teachers also empower their students to ask about the Close if one is not posted and to remind the teacher when it is time to Close on the days that the teacher is distracted while doing something important...usually teaching.

For a practical lesson planning tool, we suggest using **The Fundamental 5** Lesson Planning Template. This lesson planning template guides the teacher in building effective lessons that have all five elements of **The Fundamental 5** embedded. The tool is online and free. The lesson is generated as a Microsoft Word document that can be edited, shared, saved, and/or printed. As a bonus, the rigor and relevance of the lesson is also mapped and displayed. The tool is available on the Lead Your School website at www.leadyourschool.com. An example of how to use the template is shared below. Figure 1 is the blank template. In Figure 2, the teacher enters the state or district learning standard, the lesson Objective (written in student-friendly language), and the lesson Close (also written in student friendly language).

In Figure 3, the teacher writes out what they intend to do during the direct teach, guided practice, individual practice, and other critical parts of the lesson. Then, as shown in Figure 4, the teacher lists any lesson resources they may need and any reminders that will facilitate increased time in the Power Zone and the increased use of academic Recognition and Reinforcement. By using this lesson plan template, the teacher has a good outline of what they intend to do and accomplish during the lesson. In addition, anyone else

3

| Learning Standard(s): | Insert the state or district standard. |

Lesson Objective (Part 1 of Lesson Frame):
Rigor: Relevance: WE WILL.... (LEARN TODAY)

Lesson Activities

Direct Teach / Demonstration: My teaching and demonstration notes...
Rigor: Relevance: To Enhance Thinking & Retention: • Hands-on Activity • Talking Prompt(s) • Writing Prompt(s)

Guided Practice: What we will do during guided practice and for how long...
Rigor: Relevance: To Enhance Thinking & Retention: • Hands-on Activity • Talking Prompt(s) • Writing Prompt(s)

Individual Practice: What students will work on individually and for how long...
Rigor: Relevance: To Enhance Thinking & Retention: • Hands-on Activity • Talking Prompt(s) • Writing Prompt(s)

Other / Notes: Other activities and/or relevant information for the lesson...
Rigor: Relevance: To Enhance Thinking & Retention: • Hands-on Activity • Talking Prompt(s) • Writing Prompt(s)

Lesson Resources:

Lesson Close (Part 2 of Lesson Frame):
Rigor: Relevance: I WILL.... (EXPLAIN / SHARE / CONNECT WHAT I LEARNED TODAY)

| Power Zone Use Notes | Recognize & Reinforce Use Notes |

4

| Learning Standard(s): | Insert the state or district standard. |

Lesson Objective (Part 1 of Lesson Frame):
Rigor: Relevance: WE WILL.... (LEARN TODAY)

Lesson Activities

Direct Teach / Demonstration: My teaching and demonstration notes...
Rigor: Relevance: To Enhance Thinking & Retention: • Hands-on Activity • Talking Prompt(s) • Writing Prompt(s)

Guided Practice: What we will do during guided practice and for how long...
Rigor: Relevance: To Enhance Thinking & Retention: • Hands-on Activity • Talking Prompt(s) • Writing Prompt(s)

Individual Practice: What students will work on individually and for how long...
Rigor: Relevance: To Enhance Thinking & Retention: • Hands-on Activity • Talking Prompt(s) • Writing Prompt(s)

Other / Notes: Other activities and/or relevant information for the lesson...
Rigor: Relevance: To Enhance Thinking & Retention: • Hands-on Activity • Talking Prompt(s) • Writing Prompt(s)

Lesson Resources: GET THIS LESSON PLAN TEMPLATE FOR FREE AT LEADYOURSCHOOL.COM

Lesson Close (Part 2 of Lesson Frame):
Rigor: I WILL.... (EXPLAIN / SHARE / CONNECT WHAT I LEARNED TODAY)

| Power Zone Use Notes | Recognize & Reinforce Use Notes |
| Reminder notes... | Reminder notes... Look for... |

who may need to use this lesson plan (a substitute teacher) should have enough information to teach the lesson with some success.

Consistent Lesson Closure is not an intuitive, natural teaching practice for most teachers. It takes time and effort to make it an integrated component of pedagogy. The right routines and tools speed up the adoption process and make the implementation easier and more effective.

REASON 5:
I NEED MORE TRAINING

This constraint on consistent Lesson Closure is reasonable and understandable. Most educators want to feel completely competent and confident before trying to implement anything new in the classroom. However, in most endeavors, the initial attempts are always a little ragged, especially when compared to later attempts. As such, it is recommended that when teachers attempt to implement any new, better practice, they should refrain from judging themselves too soon. The learning curve is real, even for educators.

Learning to implement a new practice through trial and error works, but it can be both time consuming and discouraging. If the reader is fortunate enough to work in a school that provides embedded staff training throughout the school year, there is nothing wrong with requesting additional training on Lesson Closure. In fact, most school leaders will accommodate staff development requests from teachers. But do not let the real or perceived lack of training stop the attempt to implement consistent Lesson Closure. Start the practice and commit to the following basic steps.

1. Decide if students will Close with a talking or writing activity (writing is more powerful).
2. Decide if the closing prompt will address the summarization of the lesson topic or the similarities/differences of taught concepts (similarities/differences is more powerful).
3. Post the Close and read it to the class.
4. Set a timer to go off either five minutes prior to the end of class for a written Close, or three minutes prior to the end of class for a talking Close.
5. When the timer goes off, have students engage in the Close.
6. Stay in the Power Zone and monitor students as they engage in the Close.
7. While in the Power Zone, Recognize student success and Reinforce student effort.
8. Reflect on the success (or lack thereof) of the lesson.
9. Repeat every day.

The teacher who consistently follows the above steps will soon be the Lesson Closure expert on the campus. The early adopters of Lesson Closure were not formally trained on the practice. They just started, figured out the steps as they went along, and got a little better day by day.

REASON 6:
I FIND IT DIFFICULT TO COME UP
WITH NEW IDEAS FOR THE CLOSE

For teachers who have not been trained on effective Lesson Closure by LYS, this is a common roadblock.[2] At some point, every teacher would find it increasingly difficult to come up with an original Lesson Closure prompt for every lesson. Fortunately, there is no need to do this.

The closing prompt is not where teachers need to be innovative and creative. Teachers should apply their innovation and creativity for lesson delivery and lesson activities. For Lesson Closure and the closing prompt, all that is required of the teacher is to be consistent,

---

[2] Lead Your School (LYS) is the only authorized provider of **Fundamental 5** training.

effective, and efficient. In other words, they just need to use the 2 + 2 + 1 Lesson Closure formula.[3]

In an academic classroom, the first "2" of the 2 + 2 + 1 Lesson Closure formula is for the teacher to decide if students will talk or write during the Close. Either is appropriate; however, writing is more powerful. To signify to students that they will be required to talk at the end of the class, the teacher could begin the Close with *I will share with a partner...* To signify to students that they will be required to write at the end of the class, the teacher could begin the Close with *I will write...*

The second "2" of the 2 + 2 + 1 Lesson Closure formula is for the teacher to decide what students will talk or write about. The second "2" is the actual closing prompt. Again, creativity is not the goal at this point in the lesson. The goal is to maximize the effect of the Close. In this pursuit, the body of research on effective instructional practices provides a clear path. The prompt should either be a form of summarization or a form of compare and/or contrast. The teacher simply decides which of these two prompts is the best fit for the delivered lesson. Either choice is appropriate and effective; however, a compare and/or contrast Close is more powerful than a summarization Close.

---

[3] The 2 + 2 + 1 Lesson Closure formula, developed by Lead Your School, is addressed in the book, *The Fundamental 5 Revisited: Exceptional Instruction in Every Setting* (2021), by Sean Cain, Mike Laird, Sherilynn Cotten, and Jayne Ellspermann.

If a teacher were to decide on a talking Close, using the formula, one would expect to see something along the lines of *I will share with a partner how fractions and percentages are similar* or *I will share with a partner what slope represents and why it is important.* Examples of a 2 + 2 + 1 written Close could be *I will fill out a Venn Diagram on the British and Colonist views of the Boston Tea Party* or *I will write down and describe the 4 main parts of the water cycle.*

The "1" in the 2 + 2 + 1 Lesson Closure formula is for the teacher to use a timer, every lesson, every day. The timer reminds the teacher to Close the lesson and ensures there is enough time remaining in the lesson period for students to complete the Close. The use of a timer is so critical to the consistent Lesson Closure process that the author can state unequivocally, **No Timer = No Lesson Closure.**

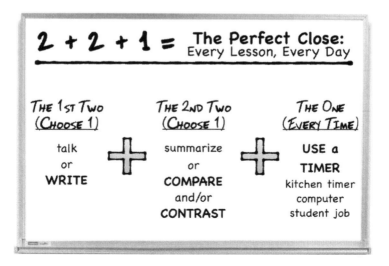

Even though the closing prompt may be similar from day to day, this really is not a compelling concern for two reasons. First, the lesson content changes day-to-day, so the answers developed and produced by students are also different day-to-day. Second, any attempt to deviate from the 2 + 2 + 1 Lesson Closure formula and add some novelty to the Close is to actually use a less effective Close. As such, teachers are encouraged to leave novelty to the less critical lesson activities and stick to the formula for Lesson Closure.

REASON 7:
IT IS DIFFICULT TO DETERMINE WHAT IS THE MOST CRITICAL IDEA/CONCEPT FROM THE LESSON

In many cases this can be true, especially when teaching a course standard that is delivered over multiple class sessions. It is also true in the classroom where, on any given day, there is some new and/or novel learning that occurs but also a lot of review and practice of prior content and skills. As a teacher and content expert, it is easy to focus on the final destination of learning (the conclusion of an instructional unit). But for the student, a content novice, the understanding of each individual component of the learning journey (each lesson) is critical if the student is to master the overall requirements of the content. As such, this begs the question, *if the teacher (a content expert) who designs and delivers the lesson cannot determine what is the most important concept, idea, or connection in the lesson, how are students (content novices) supposed to figure it out?* Though the combinations of grade levels and courses are unique, we can provide some general guidance for teachers who have this concern.

In primary grades, the daily lesson for most academic subjects has lots of embedded ongoing practice and review activities. Some of the ongoing practice and review activities are directly related to the new concept being taught today, and some are not. That is the nature of primary instruction. In this situation, the teacher should base the Close on what was taught during *Floor Time* and/or *New Teach Time*. These are the times when the teacher is teaching the new or important concept to students. This is what the teacher needs students to create a vibrant and robust memory of and what the teacher needs to immediately and formatively assess.

In English-Language Arts-Reading (ELAR) classrooms, the instructional block often has lots of embedded practice and review activities. For example, the teacher is focused on reading instruction, but there is also writing and/or grammar practice embedded in the class. The reverse also occurs when the actual lesson is focused on writing and/or grammar, but there is also some embedded reading practice that will occur. In these cases, the teacher should base the Close on the new/important information or activity that was planned for the class period (reading or writing/grammar). However, on the days that there is significant new/important information that is being taught in both areas (reading and writing/grammar), the teacher should Close the first content segment before moving on to the second content segment. The rule is if the taught content is new and/or critical, the lesson that taught that content should be Closed.

In a Workshop Model classroom (reading workshop and/or writing workshop), the teacher should base the Close on what was taught during the mini-lesson. The caveat in this classroom is that the lesson should be Closed at the end of the lesson period, not at the end of the mini-lesson. Do note, if a teacher has a block (extended time) schedule that includes both reading and writing workshops, a Close should occur at the end of the reading workshop block and another Close should occur at the end of the writing workshop block.

Finally, in a class where students are engaged in a multi-day project, students should still engage in a Close at the end of every lesson period. The Close should revolve around discussions on progress, decisions made, why decisions were made, what if different decisions were made, etc. This is done to position students to process their understanding of the project at higher levels of cognition and to facilitate their making a vibrant and robust memory of what they engaged in during the lesson. This also positions more students to meet the expectations of the teacher at the conclusion of the project.

REASON 8:
I CANNOT FIGURE OUT HOW TO MAKE LESSON CLOSURE WORK IN A PERFORMANCE CLASSROOM

First, a quick explanation/definition. There are academic and performance classrooms. In academic classrooms, the courses taught are ELAR, mathematics, science, social studies, and similar content. In performance classrooms, one will typically find art, band, career and technology, kindergarten, physical education, and similar classes being taught.

When one attempts to mimic the exact Lesson Closure practices of the academic classroom in the performance classroom, the fit can be awkward. As such, performance classroom Lesson Closure requires some slight adjustments to the practice to facilitate a seamless integration into instructional routines. From the student perspective, the purpose of Lesson Closure is to articulate the critical understanding and/or connections from the lesson and create a vibrant and robust memory while doing so. From the teacher perspective, Lesson Closure increases student retention and depth of thinking while providing the teacher with immediate formative information on the success of the lesson. This applies to both academic and performance classrooms.

In academic classrooms, the primary vehicles for Lesson Closure are a quick discussion with a partner or a quick, critical writing exercise. The student uses these vehicles when responding to the teacher's designed closing prompt. An example of the closing prompt could be *I will describe the differences between an academic and performance classroom,* and, based on the teacher's direction, students would either discuss the answer or write the answer down.

In performance classrooms, an appropriate Lesson Closure often requires the student to show something, engage in something, or demonstrate something. In other words, *perform.* Examples of a Lesson Close in a performance classroom could be *I will trace an A,* or *I will complete a straight weld,* or *I will dribble the basketball through the cones.* The teacher observes these concluding demonstrations and determines if students are making adequate progress and what will be the focus of the next class. Often, the teacher provides students with near immediate feedback on their performance, improvement, and/or level of effort.

As the understanding of effective Lesson Closure has evolved, exceptional performance teachers and coaches have added student conversation to the performance Close. Students still demonstrate the skill, but then quickly have a *why, how, feel,* or *what if* type of discussion about their performance. There are also numerous examples of performance classroom teachers who have adopted regular written Closes relating to student performance. The teachers and coaches report that there is a noticeable, accelerated improvement in student performance that they attribute to their enhanced Closing practices.

Finally, consider the group performance classroom (band, drama, choir, etc.). In the group performance classroom, the common Lesson Frame format of *We will...* for the Lesson Objective and *I will...* for the Close is often a forced fit for the planned activity. This occurs when students are working on their individual contributions to the group's performance. If this is the case, the problem is generally solved when the teacher flips the Lesson Frame. Now the *I will...* becomes the Objective and the *We will...* becomes the Close. Consider the following example used in a band class.

I will practice the beginning of my part of **The Horse**.[4] This is the Objective of today's practice session. This

---

[4] James, J. (1968). "The Horse" [Recorded by Cliff Nobles and Company]. *Love is All Right* [B-side]. Philadelphia, PA: Phil-L.A. of Soul Records.

individual practice of specific individual pieces of the performance will occupy the young musicians for most of the class period.

We will play the first part of **The Horse** *paying particular attention to the beat.* The band playing together at the end of the practice is the group performance Close. The quality of the performance provides immediate feedback to the musicians, and the band director knows exactly what will be worked on during the next practice.

As a finishing note, at the secondary level, band directors often become early adopters and advocates of appropriate Lesson Closure. As one band director explained, "Musical performances require perfection. Any practice that helps my musicians achieve perfection faster, I'm going to use."

REASON 9:
I DO NOT KNOW HOW TO CLOSE A LESSON THAT CONTINUES OVER MULTIPLE DAYS

A lesson that is delivered over multiple days is a common occurrence, especially in secondary courses on campuses where shortened class periods have become the norm. With a multiple day lesson, there are multiple Closures, a Close for the end of each class period. These interim Closes lead up to the final Close for the entire lesson.

As students progress through each day of the lesson, the teacher wants to ensure that students retain what was taught that day in order to build on that understanding the next day. The daily, interim Close within a multiple day lesson ensures that this occurs. As one progresses through a multiple day lesson, at the end of each class period summaries, comparisons, differences, decision justification, and progress discussions are all useful interim Closures. The teacher, who Closes each day of a multiple day lesson, will have more students meet the overall learning expectation of the multiple day lesson than the teacher who skips the interim Closes.

REASON 10:
I DO NOT KNOW HOW TO MAKE LESSON CLOSURE FEEL MORE AUTHENTIC OR NATURAL

This reason for not Closing the Lesson is understandable. Good teaching has a significant performance component to it, and the more "natural" the performer (teacher) feels, the better the performance (instruction). Couple this with the fact that actual, authentic Lesson Closure is exceedingly rare in the field. This means that few teachers experienced the practice when they were students. It also means that few teachers have observed other teachers using the practice.

The reader should keep in mind that most things people attempt for the first time do not feel natural and authentic. Consider riding a bicycle. For most adults, riding a bicycle is not difficult. It is a leisure and/or exercise activity that most people find enjoyable. The most natural thing in the world...or is it? Think back to what it was like when we were children and got our first real bike. Learning to ride a bike is often the first novel, weird, and scary thing that a child purposefully attempts to learn. There is absolutely nothing natural about mastering the complex machine that is a bicycle. But our parents, siblings, and friends insist that we try, so we do. Try and fail, and try and fail. We do this even when failure on a bicycle involves real fear, falling down, potential injury, and pain. But with each failure, we get back up on the bike and try again. Attempt after attempt. Day after day. Then, suddenly, it just works. We stay up and pedal, wobbly, for a couple of yards. After that, our learning curve accelerates, and within a few days, riding a bike IS the most natural thing in the world. It is as if we have been doing it forever.

Closing the Lesson works the same way. Just start doing it (see: Reason 5). It will be rough for a couple of days. It will feel clunky, and students will be confused and disinterested. You will believe that you just "crashed" a successful lesson, even though this is not the case. Then, without warning, Lesson Closure will just work. The students will no longer fight the practice, and their answers will begin to improve. Before long (within a few weeks), Lesson Closure will be such a natural occurrence that the teacher will be unable to remember a time when Closing the Lesson ever seemed difficult.

REASON 11:
I DO NOT CLOSE THE LESSON WHEN I ADMINISTER A TEST BECAUSE I DO NOT KNOW HOW TO MAKE THE PRACTICE USEFUL

This is a common statement (or question) from teachers who have had success with appropriate Lesson Closure and realize that the practice is an awkward fit on test day. There are two primary ways for a teacher to address this situation. The first approach is to reach the realization that Lesson Framing and Lesson Closure on test day is unnecessary. Test day is the one day that most students understand the objective for the day and what is expected of them—*take a test and pass the test.*

As such, the author's early advice to teachers was, "Don't worry about Lesson Framing and Lesson Closure on test day," and that was it. Even now we clearly state that on test day, Lesson Framing and Lesson Closure is an optional practice. However, not unexpectedly for teachers who have experienced the powerful positive effect that Lesson Closure has on student performance, this advice has been questioned. Because *best practice is best practice*, these teachers wanted an effective way to apply Lesson Framing and Lesson Closure in a testing environment. This ~~request~~ demand led the LYS team to a revised, better solution.

If a teacher is going to have a Lesson Frame for a test, it should be written and presented in the following manner. With the Objective, the teacher should have fun and attempt to motivate students. With the Close, the teacher should reinforce the value of effort and set a goal for students. This recommendation aligns with the body of research addressing the topics of stress, motivation, effort, and goal setting.

First the Objective. The purpose of *fun* is to reduce student stress. All things being equal, being less stressed is more conducive to performance than experiencing too much stress. Many students arrive to class on test day carrying a considerable amount of stress from a variety of sources. Recognizing this fact and working to reduce a small amount of that stress and get students to loosen up is a good coaching strategy. The purpose of *motivate* is the recognition that a motivated student will generally outperform a less motivated student with the same aptitude.

With the Close, *reinforcing the value of effort* reminds students that effort does affect outcomes. The teacher *sets a goal* because overall performance is greater with a goal than it is without a goal. For example, in a downhill skiing competition being the first skier on the course is not an advantageous position. No matter how fast the first skier is, the odds are the person will not win. Why? Because there is now a gaggle of world class skiers at the top of the mountain that now have a time to beat.

Putting this all together, for the teacher that wants to have a Lesson Frame for their test, they should write something similar to the following:

We will use our enormous brains and totally dominate the math test!

(fun and motivating)

I will work hard and score an 86 or higher on the test.

(effort reminder and goal)

One note: On the posted goal, the teacher should consider the typical student in a given class and the difficulty of the test. If 2nd period is a group of high achievers, the posted goal may be *"93 or higher."* If 3rd period is a group of struggling students, the goal may be *"78 or higher."* The idea is to position students to try and meet or exceed expectations.

REASON 12:
BASED ON WHAT OCCURRED IN CLASS MY POSTED CLOSE IS NO LONGER RELEVANT

Been there, done that. This happens to every teacher. The classroom is a complex and dynamic environment. For every element the teacher controls, there are hundreds of other things that are out of the teacher's control. Even with the best and most in-depth plans for a given lesson, every class and every day is slightly different. Sometimes students struggle with a concept more than the teacher anticipates. Sometimes a teachable moment takes the teacher in an entirely different direction. Sometimes there is a fire drill in the middle of the class period. Frankly, stuff happens. No need to panic. But there is no reason to not Close the shortened, disrupted, and/or wandering lesson.

To do this, every teacher needs to have an "Emergency Backup Close." On the days when the class period is ending and the posted Close is no longer appropriate, the teacher says, "Class, we didn't get as far as I planned. No problem, we'll get to the posted Close tomorrow. But right now, I want you to turn to your partner and discuss (insert emergency backup close here)."

To make things easier for the reader, here is the author's standard emergency backup Close: "What was the most (insert selected adjective: interesting, useful, important, weird, crazy) thing that I learned today?" With the emergency backup Close, the teacher is not concerned about what the student says or the quality of the discussion. The goal of the teacher is for students to latch on to something from the lesson and create a vibrant memory of content that can be accessed the next time the class meets.

Here is a question for the reader: does the emergency backup Close qualify as a decent Close? The answer is no. In all honesty, the emergency backup Close is less than optimal. That is why it is the emergency backup. It is like a survival meal, not really appetizing, but it will do in a pinch. However, what is a less than optimal Close always better than? No Close.

REASON 13:
STUDENTS DO NOT KNOW HOW TO ANSWER THE CLOSE

The teacher who begins to appropriately Close their Lessons quickly realizes (by *quickly* we mean usually after the first attempt) that few, if any, students are able to answer the Close correctly. This DOES NOT mean that the teacher did a poor job teaching. This DOES NOT mean that the class was not paying attention. This DOES NOT mean that Closing the Lesson did not work. Students initially struggling to respond to the Close is a natural occurrence that will improve with daily practice.

First, student confusion at the end of a lesson is not a new phenomenon. Students "did not get it" because the teacher attempted an appropriate Close. Students were not "getting it" in every previous lesson the teacher taught. But now, for the first time, the teacher knows this. This is good information.

Second, students are not accustomed to processing new information and thinking about new information in an accelerated, purposeful manner. This is an acquired skill. This is a skill that students can pick up quickly, but it is a process. As such, to eventually be successful, the teacher requires a level of patience and some faith in the process. Stick with it!

Third, once students have experience with Lesson Closure and actively engage in the daily practice, there will still be times when one, some, or all students in the class "do not get it." This is the formative information that good teachers use when making instructional decisions. Depending on the number of students who do not get it and the level of their confusion, the teacher decides how to best reteach the concept the next time the class meets. The concept(s) in question could be addressed with a warm-up activity, small group instruction, a mini-lesson, tutoring, or a full reteaching of the lesson.

Also, if this less than successful lesson is to be taught to another class that day, the teacher can make immediate delivery and/or activity adjustments in an effort to increase the number of students who do "get it" the first time. Bottom line, the teacher should not be disappointed when every student does not ace the Close—simply recognize this fact and adjust. If teaching was easy, we would not need professionals in the classroom.

REASON 14:
STUDENTS STRUGGLE WITH THE CLOSE

It is not only okay that students struggle with the Close, in most cases it should be expected. The teacher has just shared new information and taught new and novel skills and processes. The Close is generally the first, real opportunity for students to think deeply, connect, and cement that new content and understanding they have gleaned from it. This should be a struggle for most students. In fact, if the Close is not challenging for most students, then there is a good chance that the Close should have been more rigorous. This is also why the Close is a formative activity. Yes, the Close represents the end of today's lesson, but it is also a daily progress check for the overall course journey.

The teacher that notices that students have struggled with today's Close is engaging in the initial stages of real time formative assessment. The first question in this process: Why are students struggling? Is it because they are not used to paying attention in class and articulating their new understanding and connections at the end of class? If so, that is natural. Keep Closing every day, and students will grow accustomed to the new expectation. Is the struggle due to a poorly designed Close? It happens. Just write a better Close tomorrow, or better yet use the 2 + 2 + 1 Lesson Closure formula (see: Reason 6).

Once students become comfortable with the Lesson Closure process and the teacher becomes adept at writing an effective Close, the next stage of real time formative assessment can commence. The teacher uses the Close to determine the overall understanding of the lesson by the class. If the teacher determines that *all students* met the minimum expectations of the lesson, the teacher delivers the next lesson at full speed with full confidence. If the teacher determines that *most students* met the minimum expectations of the lesson, then during the next lesson after the students are released to begin the assignment, the teacher pulls the small group of struggling students to get them up to speed. If the teacher determines that essentially none of the students met the minimum expectations of the lesson, there is no need to panic. It happens. The teacher simply restates the critical point of the lesson, right then, before students exit the class. Then the next time the class meets, the teacher reteaches the concept, hopefully in a different manner.

Students are not actually struggling with the Close. Students are struggling with the taught content. The Close simply informs the teacher of this fact so the teacher can do something about it. A teacher knowing something and doing something about it is in a significantly better position than a teacher not knowing something and not responding. Unfortunately, the teacher not knowing and not responding is an ongoing reality in the classroom where appropriate and consistent Lesson Closure does not occur.

REASON 15:
STUDENTS ANSWER THE CLOSE INCORRECTLY AND LEAVE CLASS THINKING THEY ARE CORRECT

On its face, this concern seems logical and rational. But upon closer examination, the reasoning behind this concern is faulty. The first, critical question is, *Is the teacher monitoring student responses to the Close in the moment?* If the answer is no, then the brutal reality is student misunderstanding began at the start of the lesson, continued throughout the lesson, and remained at the conclusion of the lesson. The student response to the Close is a symptom of bigger instructional and pedagogical problems, *not the actual problem.*

If the teacher is monitoring how students respond to the Close, then we can consider this issue at greater depth. Yes, there are students who will engage in the Close, and it will be immediately obvious to the teacher that they did not get it. However, this is not the problem. Instead this is the answer. Students did not get the Close wrong; instead students did not glean the expected level of understanding or make the planned connections from the *lesson.*

Now that the teacher is immediately aware of this fact, they can do something to correct this very big instructional pothole. If the teacher did not have students attempt the Close, students would not have learned the critical elements of the lesson, but the teacher would be ignorant of this fact. That teacher would keep teaching forward at full speed, oblivious that they are increasing the size of the student understanding gap. For a teacher, ignorance is not bliss, it is stress in hiding.

While monitoring student responses to the Close, when the teacher realizes that students did not learn what was expected, the teacher has a couple of options for what to do next. One, if nobody got *it*, the teacher gets the class' attention and states the correct response. By doing this the teacher ensures that students leave the class a little less confused. Then, the first thing during the next class, the teacher reteaches the concept. If the teacher realizes that a few students did not get *it*, then tomorrow the teacher gets most of the class moving forward and then pulls the students that did not get it in a small group. This group of students get needed and timely additional instruction that allows them to keep pace with the rest of the class. These two strategies, which represent near immediate interventions, allow the teacher to cover more content in the long run and with greater student success. This is because the ongoing and expanding understanding gaps that plague most classrooms and drag down student performance are corrected before they can ever take hold.

REASON 16:
STUDENTS COMPLAIN ABOUT IT

For the teachers that do not Close their Lesson due to this reason, we remind them of this universal fact...students complain. For many students, the more effort and thinking required to complete a lesson activity, the more likely they are to complain. If the driving goal of a teacher is to never have students complain, then the terminal solution would be to have no work for students, no expectation of learning, and unlimited soft drinks and snacks in the classroom. This is ridiculous because even then there would be student complaints about soft drink temperature and snack selection.

Additionally, children quickly learn that if they complain loud enough and drag their feet long enough, we (teachers and most adults) will just give up and give in to their demands. This is just a short term gain in exchange for long term pain, for both the child and the adult. Early in the author's career, a veteran teacher shared the following advice: *The more students are working, the more deaf the teacher should become.* In other words, if students are engaged and working, do not worry about the complaints; it is the work that truly matters.

Close the Lesson every day. This requires students to pay attention during class at a level higher than they have grown accustomed. This requires students to think at deeper levels more often than they have grown accustomed. This is good for them. Think of students engaging in the Close as the instructional equivalent of eating their vegetables. Almost everyone has a vegetable they initially did not like but is now a favorite. Stay consistent, and before long the student complaints will diminish, the better student thinking will begin, and overall classroom performance will improve.

REASON 17:
ONCE STUDENTS BELIEVE THEY
HAVE ENOUGH INFORMATION TO
ANSWER THE CLOSE THEY QUIT

This semi-common complaint has two primary causes and a three-part cure. The first cause is that students are not accustomed to staying academically engaged throughout the entirety of the class. Though this can be a campus wide norm, in most cases it is a classroom specific concern. This means that the same student exhibits different behaviors in different classrooms, working to the end of the class for one teacher and not for another.

The second cause is that the Close is too rudimentary and lacks instructional rigor. For example, a lesson on Central American geography could have a posted Close that states, *I will list three geographic features of Mexico*. After fifteen minutes of class the student has heard or read *desert, mountain,* and *rainforest* and mentally shuts down.

The three-part cure is teacher expectation, practice, and time. First, the teacher must create and reinforce the *expectation* that students will engage in academic activities for the entire class period. Second, the teacher should work to create more challenging and academically rigorous closing prompts (see: Reason 6). The more *practice* the teacher has writing closing prompts and the more *practice* students have responding to the Close, the better everyone becomes with the process. Finally, the teacher must exhibit persistence and patience. The more consecutive days the teacher has the students engage in the Close and then writes a new closing prompt after reflecting on the results to the previous closing prompt—*practice and time*—the more effective and efficient the Closing process becomes. When the class reaches the point where the daily engagement in the Close is effective, efficient, and produces noticeable improvement in student retention and understanding, the teacher's *expectation* will be met. Thus, completing the expectation, practice, and time loop.

REASON 18:
I AM CONCERNED ABOUT STUDENT
BEHAVIOR IF I LET THEM TALK AT
THE END OF CLASS

This is a legitimate concern. Let us be honest. For too many years and at too many campuses, poor student behavior in the classroom garners significantly more negative attention by administration than poor academic performance by students in the class. In that same spirit of honesty, we must also admit that academically engaged students behave better than academically disengaged students. This is why exceptional teachers know that the best student behavior management strategy is keeping as many students as possible cognitively engaged with content for as long as possible.

Put a pin in that fact as we consider another fact. As humans, we have an innate compulsion to talk. In too many classrooms, teachers enforce a "no talking" rule, purposefully shutting down any talk that the teacher did not explicitly allow. For many students, this makes the natural urge to talk even more compelling and difficult to restrain. What is interesting is that this need to talk is not necessarily topic driven. This means that the topic of the talk is generally less important than the act of talking. The practical application of this interesting fact is that the teacher can use student academic talk as a behavior management tool.

Let us take these two facts, (a) engaged students are better behaved, and (b) using student talk for an instructional purpose to manage behavior, and consider the teacher practices that leverage this knowledge. Peeking in a classroom, we observe a teacher who has their students working on an assignment during the period. As students attend to their work, the clock continues to tick and their feeling for the need to talk to someone increases but remains stifled. As the class is wrapping up, the need to talk becomes almost overwhelming for a number of students. Then the teacher says, "Before we leave, turn to your partner and share how the differences between the primary and secondary characters of this story impact their relationship."

The teacher is implementing a talking Close. The students turn to their partners and begin to talk, and talk they do because it is meeting their needs. But the talk is academic, and conversations are meeting an instructional intent…if the teacher remains in the Power Zone to monitor the conversations. Yes, the behavior could be a little ragged, at first. Yes, it is probable that a student or two will talk off topic. But the more Lesson Closure becomes the routine, student behavior, thinking, retention, and performance will all improve. If students lack the requisite skill and focus to engage in a quality talking Close, all is not lost. In grades 3-12 academic classes, a written Close is always appropriate and is more powerful than a talking Close. Problem solved.

REASON 19:
ONCE STUDENTS START TO GET READY FOR THE BELL I CANNOT RECAPTURE THEIR ATTENTION

This is a real problem on campuses where students have become accustomed to not engaging in classwork until the end of the period, regardless of the reason. The problem is solved by creating and teaching a new classroom routine. The teacher should communicate to students at the beginning of class what will occur during the class period, what the teacher expects students to do during the class period, what this will look like, and that the teacher will let them know when to get ready for dismissal.

Then the teacher should do exactly what they told the students would occur. During the Close, when old student habits are likely to re-emerge, the teacher should be in the Power Zone monitoring student engagement.

While monitoring students, the teacher should stay in close proximity to the students most likely to disengage and provide verbal reinforcement and encouragement to any and every student that warrants it. Most students will adapt to the new expectation and Closing routine in a timely fashion (a couple of days of consistent implementation by the teacher).

Some classes may need to experience some mild consequences to change their behavior. The class may need to experience the universal reality that the teacher dismisses the class, not the bell. The teacher may need to count the student's engagement in the Close as a participation grade, or the teacher may use yesterday's Closing question as a one question pop quiz at the beginning of today's class. However, as is the case in the use of any negative classroom consequence, the teacher should not make the consequence so severe that a student cannot recover quickly.

Finally, if the reader is the only teacher appropriately Closing the Lesson, it will take longer for the students to adapt to the new routine. But if the entire school is working to consistently implement Lesson Closure, the quicker one would expect students to get on board. A teacher consistently Closing the Lesson is the exercise and performance equivalent to jogging a mile every day. An entire staff consistently Closing the Lesson is the exercise and performance equivalent to sprinting a mile every day. The latter allows one to achieve the desired result in less time.

REASON 20:
WHEN STUDENTS HEAR THE TIMER THEY TUNE OUT BECAUSE "CLASS IS OVER"

The teachers dealing with this reason have a situation similar to Reason 19. This issue is best addressed by creating new classroom routines and habits. The good news is this teacher is using a timer to ensure that they Close the Lesson. Using a timer is a solid time management practice that all teachers should adopt. The adjustment to practice is that the teacher should use their timer for more than just signaling Lesson Closure.

The timer should be used to signal every significant lesson transition that occurs during the class period. The timer should signal when the time allotted for the warm-up has expired. The timer should be used to ensure that the time allotted for the direct teaching component of the lesson does not infringe on student practice time. The timer can be used to signal when guided practice should transition to group practice and when group practice should transition to individual practice. Finally, as the class period is concluding, the timer signals when to set aside all other lesson activities and engage in today's Lesson Closure.

The use of a timer is a commonly observed practice in successful early primary classrooms, reading and writing workshop classrooms, classrooms serving students with special needs, and athletic programs. The students in these settings represent all ages, grade levels, ability levels, and motivation levels. Any negative classroom management issues relating to the use of a timer are not actually timer issues. They are instead expectation and routine issues. If students have previously been taught in classrooms that do not regularly use timers, then over time their behavior has been modified to equate a ringing bell with the end of class. The more a timer is used appropriately throughout a class period, the more students connect the sound of the timer to *transition* or *change* instead of *quit and leave*. The solution is not to abandon the timer, but to teach, model, and reinforce the new expectation and routine.

REASON 21:
I NEED TIME FOR STUDENTS TO
CLEAN UP AND GET READY TO LEAVE

The validity of this constraint is dependent on the type of activity for the day and/or the course being taught. In the typical academic classroom with the typical instructional activity, no more than a minute or two is required to prepare to transition to another subject or leave the class. Kindergarten students are often observed putting up their materials and preparing to transition to another activity in less than a minute. Secondary teachers are often observed having students engaged in academic activities until the bell rings and then students clean up their workspace and put up class materials as they exit the classroom. This is done within the standard five minute passing period. The point being that smooth and efficient cleanup and transition practices are a product of focused, purposeful routines.

However, there are activities and classes that create "messes" that require more time to clean up, put up, and/or organize prior to the students leaving class. An art class is one such example, another could be a construction technology class. When the cleanup process requires more than a minute or two, we recommend that the teacher use a talking Close. Students are going to talk as they clean up. Any attempt to prevent this is essentially futile. The trick is to lean into it. Have the students talk about the work they just completed—*a talking Close*—instead of engaging in idle chit-chat and gossip as they clean up. This is a Win-Win-Win.

WIN, the room is cleaned, organized, and prepared for the next class. **WIN**, the students compelling need to talk is satisfied (see: Reason 18). **WIN**, the Close is engaged in and completed, increasing student retention and understanding of the just completed lesson/activity.

REASON 22:
I HAVE TOO MUCH INFORMATION TO COVER

To address this concern, the teacher must prioritize the value of the different elements of information shared in any given lesson. As content experts, it is easy to fall into the trap of believing that every bit of content information that is intended to be shared in a lesson is equally important. It is not. Or at least not everything is equally important to the novice, which is what students are.

A primary responsibility of teachers and lesson designers is to make sure that students are exposed to the critical content information and to deliver that critical content information in a way that ensures the greatest degree of retention. When this is done effectively and efficiently, each lesson builds on the next, positioning students to think deeper about the material and/or better use the material.

In this endeavor, Lesson Closure is an invaluable tool. A two-to-three minute turn and talk Close at the end of the lesson creates a vibrant and robust memory of the critical information and connections from the lesson that the students just experienced. A three-to-five minute written Close makes that vibrant and robust memory more tangible and concrete. As students build on robust memory after robust memory, their understanding of the content grows at an accelerated pace. This in turn allows a teacher who consistently Closes the Lesson to cover more content, often at greater depth and complexity, than the teacher who does not Close the Lesson. Hence, the more content a teacher is required to cover during a school year, the more critical the practice of consistent and appropriate Lesson Closure becomes (see: Reason 1).

REASON 23:
I AM TRYING TO STAY ON PACE WITH THE SCOPE AND SEQUENCE

Hooray! Staying on pace with the scope and sequence is one of the most powerful practices available to teachers in their pursuit of maximizing student opportunities and improving student performance.[5] All things being equal, the students who see more course content during the year have a competitive advantage over their peers who are exposed to less course content during the same time period.

Additionally, in today's high-stakes accountability education environment, the need for a teacher to move through curriculum at an accelerated pace is magnified. The pressure to stay on pace with the scope and sequence

---

[5] The power and impact of scope and sequence fidelity is addressed in the book, *The Classroom Playbook: The Power of a Common Scope and Sequence* (2020), by Sean Cain and Mike Laird.

is real and legitimate. Due to monitored (both internally and externally) content pacing requirements, Closing the Lesson is not just a good idea, it is mission critical.

Closing the Lesson appropriately has a significant positive impact on student retention. However, this positive impact is not immediately noticeable to the teacher. As such, on any given day, the practice may seem as if it is slowing the teacher down. The teacher feels as if Closing the Lesson is robbing them of a precious three-to-five minutes to share just one last thing. On the micro-level, this could even be true. But the reader/teacher should consider the macro-level view.

If a teacher does NOT Close the Lesson appropriately, students will NOT retain as much of the content taught that day as they could. When these students return to class the next day, due to the lack of retention of the previous day's content, the teacher must review prior content in order to effectively teach any new content. This review of prior content takes time. The more time that is spent on review, the less time there is available for new content teaching. When the teacher Closes the Lesson appropriately, students are positioned to retain more of the content the teacher taught that day. When these same students return to class the next day, because they remember more of the previous day's lesson, less review of prior content is required. This provides the teacher with more time to teach more new content. The math is simple, clear, and inescapable.

No Lesson Closure = 3 extra minutes devoted to review and clarification, per day

No Lesson Closure = 15 extra minutes devoted to review and clarification, per week

No Lesson Closure = 270 extra minutes devoted to review and clarification, per semester

No Lesson Closure = 540 extra minutes devoted to review and clarification, per year

Lesson Closure = 12 additional days devoted to new content instruction, per year*

* Based on a 45-minute class period and a 180 day school year.

On any given day, this time discrepancy between the teacher who Closes the Lesson consistently and the teacher who does not barely registers with either teacher. But project this difference in available new content delivery time over the course of a month, a semester, or a year, and the results get increasingly dramatic. The teacher who Closes the Lesson consistently can cover more content and with greater student performance than the teacher who does not Close the Lesson consistently. Simply put, the teacher who does not Close the Lesson consistently (or at all) everyday falls further and further behind. The teacher who Closes the Lesson consistently is better able to stay on pace with the scope and sequence.

REASON 24:
I NEED TO SHARE ONE MORE THING OR STUDENTS NEED TO DO ONE MORE PRACTICE PROBLEM

This common reason is the one the author understands the most and still struggles with when teaching and presenting. The need to share one more thing and have students complete one more practice problem is embedded in my math teacher DNA. After all, the typical teacher is passionate about their content area and wants all their students to experience the joy of mastering a favorite subject.

As content experts, we know more information than we can share in an allotted amount of time. Couple this with the fact that teachers generally present information in a logical and linear fashion, building on prior knowledge and understandings. This means that the next thing a teacher wants to share with the class is, at that moment, more important and critical than anything shared previously. What we have to remind ourselves is that hearing information and understanding information are not the same thing. The effective teacher has the discipline to stop talking and provide students with processing and connection opportunities that turn information into knowledge. This is what occurs when students are provided enough time to engage in the Close.

Like many teachers, the author understands that one of the secrets of academic success is doing the work. This is then conflated into the belief that students must engage in skill and process practice problems up until the bell rings. When compared to not doing practice problems, an entire class period spent doing practice problems does add value. As recent as 20 years ago (when many current teachers were students), that was the limit of "best" practice. Now we know better.

Skip making one last point. Skip the last two practice problems. Instead have the class engage in a Close that connects what they learned to something else, summarizes key understandings, and/or provides meaning and context. This promotes deeper learning and increased retention. In turn, this means that tomorrow, instead of the teacher needing to review what was covered in the last lesson, the teacher can move the class forward and teach more new material.

REASON 25:
I DO NOT WANT TO LOSE THE TEACHING MOMENT I AM IN SO I JUST TEACH TO THE BELL

This is understandable. Everything is flowing, the teacher is on a roll, and the students are engaged. For most teachers this experience is just rare enough that they want to savor it and not waste it. But by teaching right to the bell and not Closing the Lesson, that is exactly what the teacher did, wasted the experience and squandered the moment.

The students did not get the chance to articulate the key understandings or connections made during the awesome lesson in which they just participated. All they have time to do is nod their heads in affirmation of what the teacher just shared. They do this as they scamper out of the room, heading to the next class before the tardy bell rings, just like every other day.

When the students return to class the next day, they do not quite remember what they were taught yesterday. The previous special teaching moment that the teacher enjoyed has become a quickly fading student memory. No teacher should let this happen to them. Embrace those special teaching moments when they occur and treat them with the esteem they deserve by stopping with enough time for students to engage in the Close. When the teacher does this, students will create a vibrant and robust memory of an incredible lesson delivered by a teacher *in a zone*.

REASON 26:
STUDENTS ARE BUSY FINISHING
THEIR ASSIGNMENTS

This is another understandable teacher roadblock to consistent Lesson Closure. As a profession, we teachers are very task oriented. If the assignment has fifteen questions, then fifteen questions should be completed by the end of class. In addition to this internal teacher motivation, "bell-to-bell" instruction has been the mantra of almost every school administrator for the past forty years. Finally, every veteran teacher intuitively understands three things about classwork.

1. The more work a student completes, the better the student retains the skills and/or information being taught.
2. A student hard at work is a well-behaved student.

CLOSE LIKE A BOSS

3.   Students distracted from their work have a
difficult time refocusing and completing their
work.

As such, purposefully stopping on-task and focused
students who have yet to complete their assignments
seems misguided. But it is not.

Yes, teachers want students to work diligently on
their assignments. But let us remember why teachers want
this to occur…so students can learn and retain
information. When a teacher does not Close the Lesson
appropriately, engagement in learning activities may
occur, but the long-term retention of the content is
significantly degraded. It then begs the question, *If students
do not remember the information, did they really learn it?*

REASON 27:
I AM EXPECTED TO TEACH BELL-TO-BELL

Yes, almost without exception, there is an expectation that teachers will teach bell-to-bell. But teaching bell-to-bell does not mean that the teacher is talking or demonstrating for the entire class period. Teaching bell-to-bell means that the teacher has students engaged in meaningful academic activities for the entire class period. Any definition to the contrary is purposefully obtuse. Closing the Lesson is not a case of not teaching bell-to-bell. Closing the Lesson is teaching bell-to-bell in the most effective manner possible.

Consider the typical teacher. This teacher starts the class, teaches and/or demonstrates something, and then gets students working on an assignment. The teacher monitors student performance and reminds them to keep working as their effort and attention ebbs. Then the bell rings and the class is over. For the typical teacher, the instructional mission has been accomplished, and typical student performance results are to be expected.

Do not be typical; be slightly atypical. Start the class, teach and demonstrate something, and then get students working on the assignment, typical. Monitor performance and encourage students to keep trying as their effort and attention ebbs, typical. Everything seems ordinary until the last five minutes of class. At this point, tell the students to get to a stopping point on their assignment. Then have every student engage in the Close—atypical!

Teaching and learning are still occurring, except now at a higher level. Students who engage in an appropriate Close retain more information than students that do not engage in a Close. This means that with just a small change in instructional delivery and student activity in the last five minutes of class, the now atypical teacher begins to get atypical results in student performance. This is a win for the teacher and potentially life changing for students.

REASON 28:
I FEEL TOO MUCH PRESSURE TO
ALWAYS HAVE A PERFECT CLOSE

Without question, many teachers are perfectionists. As such, it is easy for those teachers to put undue pressure on themselves to always have the perfect Close. Also, when perfectionists try something new, as the old joke highlights, their inner critic has a critic. We advise teachers to let go of the feeling that the Close must be perfect. Instead embrace the process of working towards perfection.

It is true that a mythical *perfect* Close is better than a less than perfect Close. However, a less than perfect Close is infinitely better than something. The something? No Close. It is cliché to say that *Good is the Enemy of Great.* But in day-to-day classroom operations, especially when attempting to adopt and master new instructional practices, teachers should not let *Perfect Prevent Progress.*

Our perfectionist teachers are encouraged to teach their lesson as they have always done, then use an initial, okay Close (see: Reason 6). By doing so, students will remember more of what they were taught. Then, on the next day, teach and Close again, and again, and again. The more the teacher engages in the practice of Lesson Closure, the better they will get, and the better students will respond. The learning curve is real, even for perfectionists (see: Reason 5 and Reason 10). Just engage and remember—real perfectionists do not quit. They keep working at the task until they meet their own internal standard.

REASON 29:
IT IS OVERWHELMING – ONE MORE THING ON TOP OF TOO MANY OTHER THINGS

~~This situation could be true~~. There is no doubt that this is a true statement. Yet the following is also true. Closing the Lesson consistently and appropriately is one of the most powerful retention practices available to a teacher. When compared to not Closing the Lesson, the performance benefits of consistent Lesson Closure are real, noticeable, and extraordinary. Yes, Lesson Closure may be one more new thing, but in the typical classroom, it is the most important new thing.

Two considerations. First, for teachers to engage in a new, better instructional practice, they should let go of an older, ineffective practice. Both instructional leaders and teachers often forget this. Not Closing the lesson is an ineffective practice, but it requires no work or effort on the part of the teacher...or does it? Yes, Closing the Lesson is adding some teacher work at the end of the period. But over time it will reduce a lot of typical teacher tasks. When a teacher consistently implements Lesson Closure, students retain more of the taught content. This means that the need to reteach prior content throughout the year is reduced. This means that the need for extensive content review prior to tests is reduced. When students retain more of what was taught, their grades improve. The more students passing the teacher's class, the fewer parent phone calls the teacher must make (at least the uncomfortable ones), and the fewer parent meetings and student staffings the teacher must attend.

Second, as stated repeatedly, Lesson Closure is a powerful retention practice. The more a teacher attempts this practice, the better the teacher and students get at it. This, in turn, drives increased student retention and mastery of the content. Over time, this has a significant positive impact on student performance, which should significantly reduce teacher stress and anxiety.

No one can do everything all the time. As such, we remind the teachers dealing with this anxiety to attempt to relax and give themselves a small break. Then do the most powerful things (see: **The Fundamental 5,** Lesson Closure) and the effects of not doing the less critical things will become increasingly inconsequential.

REASON 30:
I FEEL LIKE I WOULD BE CLOSING THE LESSON JUST SO AN OBSERVER CAN CHECK IT OFF ON A LIST

If Framing the Lesson with Appropriate Lesson Closure is a campus focus, then yes, there is a strong possibility that campus leadership will look for evidence that the practice is being implemented when they visit the classroom. So what? Looking for evidence of the implementation of high-yield instructional practices is the purpose of a classroom observation.

However, regarding the "checking off the list" feeling, it must be pointed out that the frequency of classroom observations in the last three-to-five minutes of a class period is microscopically low. This means that a teacher being constrained due to this reason or feeling is sacrificing one of the most powerful student retention practices in their instructional tool box—every period, every day—just on the off chance that they might demonstrate to campus leadership that they are using a specific instructional practice that makes them a better teacher.

Now, if like all of us, the teacher is feeling a little belligerent because they believe they are being forced to do something that has little value, that feeling is misguided...but completely understandable. The practice of Lesson Closure may be new or uncomfortable to a teacher. When first attempting to implement the practice, the positive results are negligible (few things in life are immediately effective the first time). As such, this is where some professional trust and faith are required. First, the teacher has to trust that campus leadership is putting in place a practice that makes teachers more effective, no matter how uncomfortable the practice may initially seem. Second, the teacher has to have some faith that given time, they will improve at the practice, which will then drive a positive change in student performance. Without this professional trust and faith, there is no hope for improvement; there is only the continued erosion of the status quo. Finally, does it truly matter why a best practice is implemented? It does not because the underlying equation is as follows: **an implemented best practice** + *any reason* = **an implemented best practice**.

REASON 31:
I EXPECT STUDENTS TO DISCOVER UNDERSTANDING AND DO NOT BELIEVE THAT SPOON FEEDING UNDERSTANDING IS PRODUCTIVE

This is the objection to consistent Lesson Closure from the discovery lesson advocate. First, we must state that 100% solutions are rare in the field of education. As soon as one says, *this is it, forever and always*, the pesky exception will inevitably arrive. With Lesson Closure, the discovery lesson is the semi-exception. However, we must also recognize that regardless of how effective the discovery lesson may be, it, too, is not a 100% solution. At best, the discovery lesson is a 10% solution.

Standard Lesson Framing procedure is for the teacher (the content expert) to write the Objective and Close on the board and verbally share the Lesson Frame with the students at the beginning of class. This informs students (the content novices) of what is expected of them at the end of the lesson and provides students with a mental filter to process and sort instructional information throughout the lesson.

In a discovery lesson, the teacher expects students (again, the content novices) to process the instructional information of the lesson, make appropriate connections throughout the lesson, and arrive at the central understanding of the lesson, with little or no direction or assistance. This type of lesson has its place in a classroom…occasionally. The discovery lesson may be an effective way to teach some students, but it is not an efficient way to teach all students. The more a teacher relies on discovery lessons, the greater the disadvantage to the students who arrive to the class without a lot of background knowledge, life experience, and/or intrinsic motivation. This can make the job of the teacher teaching a high-stakes accountability course exceedingly more difficult and stressful.

Regardless, at the end of a discovery lesson, the teacher should still Close the Lesson. A quick write exit ticket or a quick partner talk will suffice. This teacher-planned-but surprise-to-the-student Close will ensure that the students who made the correct discovery will better retain what they discovered. The teacher will also be able to immediately identify the students who did not make the correct discovery, so they will be prepared to reteach the concept to the struggling students the next day. Not

Closing a discovery lesson results in the teacher operating blind, an unknown number of students not discovering the understanding, and the students who did discover the understanding quickly forgetting what they discovered. This is not a case of spoon feeding student understanding, this is a case of wasting teacher and student time and effort.

CONCLUSION

On paper, Closing the Lesson is a simple concept. With three-to-five minutes remaining in class, have students put aside the academic task they are working on and respond to a posted closing prompt. A closing prompt that either positions students to articulate the key understanding from the lesson they just participated in or the key connections they made. Students do this quickly and informally, usually by talking to a partner or completing a quick write. Then they go to the next class. When students respond to the Close, retention is increased, understanding is solidified, and over time academic performance improves. When teachers ask what is the one thing they can do to improve student performance, the answer is *Close the Lesson*.

As it is with many things, simple on paper proves to be difficult in practice. Habit, routine, and comfort drive a lot of classroom practices. As teachers, we do the things that we experienced when we were students, we do the things that we have done many times before, and we avoid the things that cause discomfort. The cause of the Lesson Closure implementation challenge is that Lesson Closure checks none of those boxes.

The previous generation of teachers—our teachers—did not Close the Lesson in the way that we now know is effective. This was not negligence; it is simply the recognition that the understanding of effective Lesson Closure has advanced in recent years. For the teachers that taught us, teaching to the bell was a high-yield practice. Just as the teacher telling their students what was just taught was a high-yield practice. Now we know how to conclude a lesson and lesson period—*better.*

For this generation of teachers, Closing the Lesson is the new, better practice. It is a practice that we have not done before, which means that it is not an already existing instructional habit. This makes the implementation of the practice difficult...but not impossible. All that is required is an understanding of how to build a new habit and some support.

Three things are required to build a new habit. A replacement behavior, a behavioral cue, and a reinforcer. Let us use this framework and apply it to Lesson Closure. First, there are four replacement behaviors required for consistent Lesson Closure, which adds complexity to the implementation endeavor. The teacher needs to develop a Close prior to the class (1). This requires a slight change to the lesson planning process. Then the teacher needs to write the Close prominently on their presentation board, visible to all in the class (2). This requires reorganizing the presentation board and removing less critical information. Then the teacher needs to set a timer to let everyone in the class know when it is time to Close (3). This requires having a timer. If the first three replacement behaviors occur, then when the timer goes off, the teacher Closes the Lesson (4).

Second, the teacher needs a behavioral cue, something that reminds them to do the replacement behavior at the appropriate time. The cue for creating a Close for a lesson could be an added space or line on a lesson plan form (see: Reason 4). The cue for writing the Close on the presentation board could be a prominent and adequately sized space on the presentation board (see: Reason 4). The cue for setting the timer could be to place the timer in a location where it is always visible. If the teacher downloads a timer to their computer, the timer can be programmed to always go off at set times (this is the recommended practice). The cues for actually Closing the Lesson are the Close, prominently posted on the board, and the timer going off three-to-five minutes prior to the end of class.

Third, the teacher needs to recognize the reinforcers for engaging in the replacement behaviors. The reinforcer for building the Close for a lesson is the completed lesson plan form. An empty space on the lesson plan form means the task was not completed. A filled space means that the task was completed, which feels good. The reinforcer for writing the Close on the board is seeing the Close on the board. The teacher knows they are making progress towards Closing the Lesson, and they also know if an observer enters the room the observer will notice the prominently posted Close. The reinforcer for setting the timer is the relief they feel knowing that they did not forget this critical step. The initial reinforcer for Closing the Lesson is the feeling of accomplishment one gets for actually doing a new thing, even if it did not work exactly as planned. The last and most powerful reinforcer for Lesson Closure is when students become accustomed to the process and when most of them successfully respond to the Close on most days.

There are a lot of moving parts required to consistently implement this high-yield practice in the classroom. As such, the more support a teacher has access to in this endeavor, the greater the chance for consistent Lesson Closure becoming a reality. Initially, a better lesson planning tool and regular team instructional planning goes a long way. Next, having a method to better organize one's presentation board, and campus leadership's encouragement to do so, removes a significant implementation hurdle (see: Reason 4). Instead of managing a timer, yet one more thing for a busy teacher to do, make being the class timekeeper a student job. Other adults that visit the classroom can be a great support. From providing feedback and suggestions on the quality of the closing prompt, to cueing the teacher to engage in the Close, to assisting in the managing and monitoring of the process when students are first introduced to the procedure. Finally, the most powerful support for teachers attempting to implement consistent Lesson Closure in their classroom is the students. Let students know that the Close is for them and empower them to ask what today's Close will be if it is not posted on the board. Tell students it is okay to remind the teacher when it is time to Close if (or when) the teacher loses track of time. When they do so, thank them.

Yes, the practice of Lesson Closure can be ragged and uncomfortable at first. Expect this and work through the minor setbacks and adversity. With just a small dose of perseverance, the initial discomfort dissolves and Lesson Closure quickly turns into a new, powerful instructional practice and classroom routine. In the course of transforming this high-yield instructional practice into a consistent classroom routine, we suggest the following implementation timeline. For the first three weeks of implementation, use a talking Close. With early primary grades and performance classrooms, the talking

Close will remain the Closing vehicle of choice in most cases. In grades 3-12 academic courses, continue to cultivate the practice of Lesson Closure with the following progression. During weeks 4-6, implement one written Close per week. During weeks 7-9, implement two written Closes per week. After week 9, implement three written Closes a week, with Friday being a mandatory written Close day. This progression builds the routine, builds the student skill set, and creates a Closing and writing culture for the entire campus.

Most days when a student is asked what they learned that day, the answer is invariably, "Nothing." With more prodding, the student usually struggles to come up with something of substance to share but generally fails. This is called *exposure with no Closure*. The student was engaged in schoolwork all day long, but there

CLOSE LIKE A BOSS!

Fundamentals	2 + 2 + 1: Expanded
☑ "I will…" Statement	☑ Why…
☑ Written BIG and Easy to Read	☑ Justify…
☑ Proof of Understanding	☑ Explain…
☑ Provides Formative Info	☑ What If…
☑ Every Student Participates	☑ How Do You Know…
☑ Every Lesson… Every Day	☑ Other Ways…

were no opportunities to cement understanding and create vibrant or robust memories of content. When a teacher Closes the Lesson, they position that student to create vibrant memories about content. The next time this student is asked what they learned in school today, they might say, "In math I learned about this slopey thing that looks like a slide." It may not be much, but it is a start, and it is a whole lot better than "Nothing."

ABOUT THE AUTHOR

Sean Cain is the co-author of:

- *The Fundamental 5: The Formula for Quality Instruction*
- *The Classroom Playbook: The Power of a Common Scope and Sequence*
- *The Reboot: School Operations in an Unpredictable World*
- *The Reboot Classroom: Teacher Decisions in the Time of COVID-19*
- *The Fundamental 5 Revisited: Exceptional Instruction in Every Setting*

Sean Cain spent the formative years of his career working in difficult instructional settings. Recognized for the success of his students and the systems he designed and implemented, he quickly progressed through the instructional leadership ranks. This culminated in his last public education position as State Director of Innovative School Redesign (Texas). Currently, Cain serves as the Chief Idea Officer for Lead Your School (LYS), a confederation of successful school leaders dedicated to improving student, campus, and district performance. A passionate speaker, Cain is a sought after national presenter and trains educators in school districts across the country. The co-author of several popular books addressing school operations and classroom instruction, he is known for his ability to make complex problems solvable and transform theory into actionable practice.